The Red Blanket

BY Eliza Thomas

ILLUSTRATED BY Joe Cepeda

SCHOLASTIC PRESS   NEW YORK

To PanPan —E.T.

For our baby in the sky —J.C.

LIBRARY OF CONGRESS CATALOGING-IN-PUBLICATION DATA

Thomas, Eliza.

The red blanket / by Eliza Thomas; illustrated by Joe Cepeda. — 1st ed.   p. cm.

Summary: Tells the story of a single woman who goes to China to adopt a baby.

ISBN 0-439-32253-7

[1. Intercountry adoption—Fiction. 2. Adoption—Fiction. 3. Single-parent families—Fiction.] I. Cepeda, Joe, ill. II. Title. PZ7.T36662Re 2004   [E]—dc21   2003005082

10 9 8 7 6 5 4   06 07 08

Printed in Singapore 46

First edition, May 2004

The illustrations were painted in oil. The display type was set in Steam. The text type was set in Hoefler Text.

Book design by Marijka Kostiw

Author's Note

The Red Blanket is an expanded version of the adoption story I first began telling my daughter, PanPan, when she was three years old. I wanted her to learn about our family history in a way that was tangible and familiar, and her beloved red blanket was the obvious place to start.

I traveled to China in 1994 to adopt PanPan. I was a first-time parent at age 46, while she, at five months, had lived in an orphanage almost since birth. As mother and daughter, we were both inexperienced, sailing in uncharted territory. Our first weeks and months together were wonderful, joyous, terrifying, confusing, magical, and exhausting. Love is effortless at times, and hard-won at others. But the soft baby blanket I had brought with me to China — and the simple act of giving it to my daughter — comforted and reassured us both, and embodied the beginning of our connection.

For years, PanPan carried the red blanket with her everywhere. It is now a web of ragged strands and knots, unrecognizable as a blanket, but it remains one of her most valuable possessions.

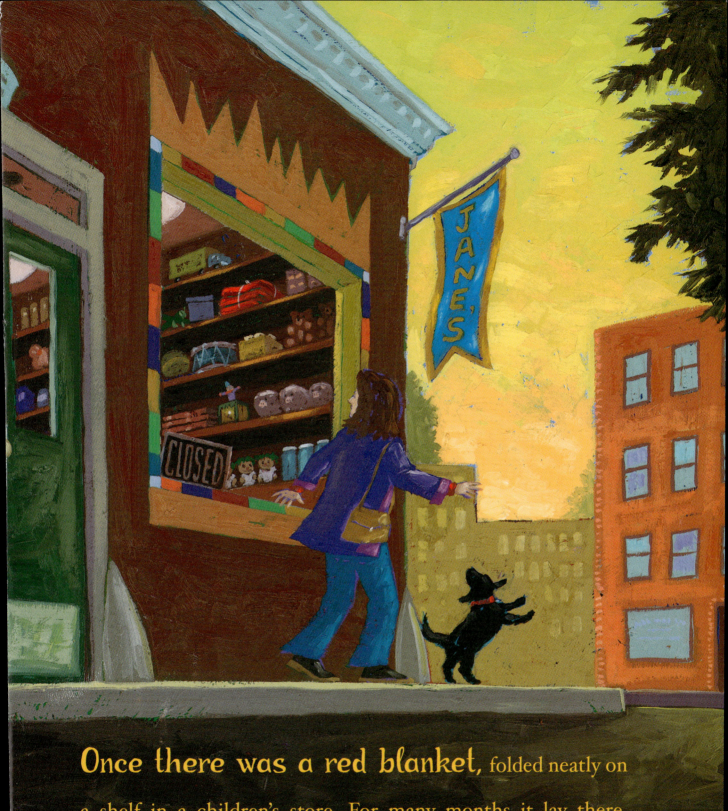

Once there was a red blanket, folded neatly on a shelf in a children's store. For many months it lay there, almost forgotten. It was the perfect size for a small child.

I lived with my dog, Lily, a few miles from town. Apple trees grew in my front yard, and there was a pond across the road. The house was filled with pictures to look at and books to read and even a beautiful piano I played every day. But still, it felt empty. I loved Lily, and she went everywhere with me. Still, I felt a little lonely. I was sad that I had no children.

One evening, I was sitting on the back porch with Lily. Somewhere, a little girl is waiting for a mommy, I thought. There *must* be a way to bring us together. I rubbed Lily's soft ears. I thought late into the night.

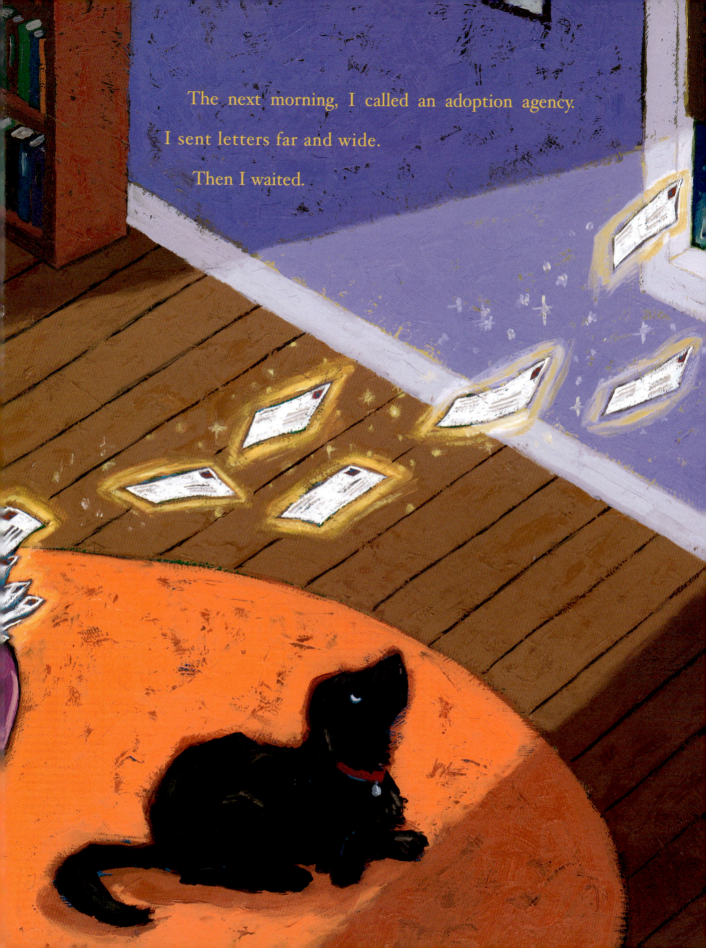

The next morning, I called an adoption agency.

I sent letters far and wide.

Then I waited.

Deep snows fell, then melted into a muddy spring. I dreamed about my baby. Summer came and went, and the mornings grew crisp and cool. I longed to see my baby's face, to hold my baby's hand in mine.

There were tiny apples on the trees in the yard when, at last, a letter arrived. My hands were trembling as I opened the envelope. Inside was a small photograph — a baby girl with shining eyes and a thatch of black hair. The letter told me her name was PanPan. She lived in an orphanage on the outskirts of a city in China. "Please come soon," the letter said.

Yes! I was so excited that I jumped up and down all around the yard.

"Hooray!" cheered our friends and neighbors.

"Woof!" said Lily.

I raced into town to the children's store. I bought diapers and baby bottles and milk formula. I bought white T-shirts and yellow pants, striped pajamas and tiny green socks. I found a rattle and a little brown bear. What else will my baby need? I wondered anxiously.

Then, just as I was about to leave the store, I noticed the blanket, all alone on a high shelf. I took it down. "I'd like to buy this, too," I told the store clerk.

At home, I packed everything into my suitcase, folding the red blanket carefully in a corner. I was ready to go.

I brought Lily to a friend's house and kissed her good-bye. "Be a good dog," I said. Lily looked worried. "I'll be back soon, with PanPan. You'll see."

I kissed her again and she wagged her tail. Then I went to the airport, boarded an enormous airplane, and flew all the way across the ocean.

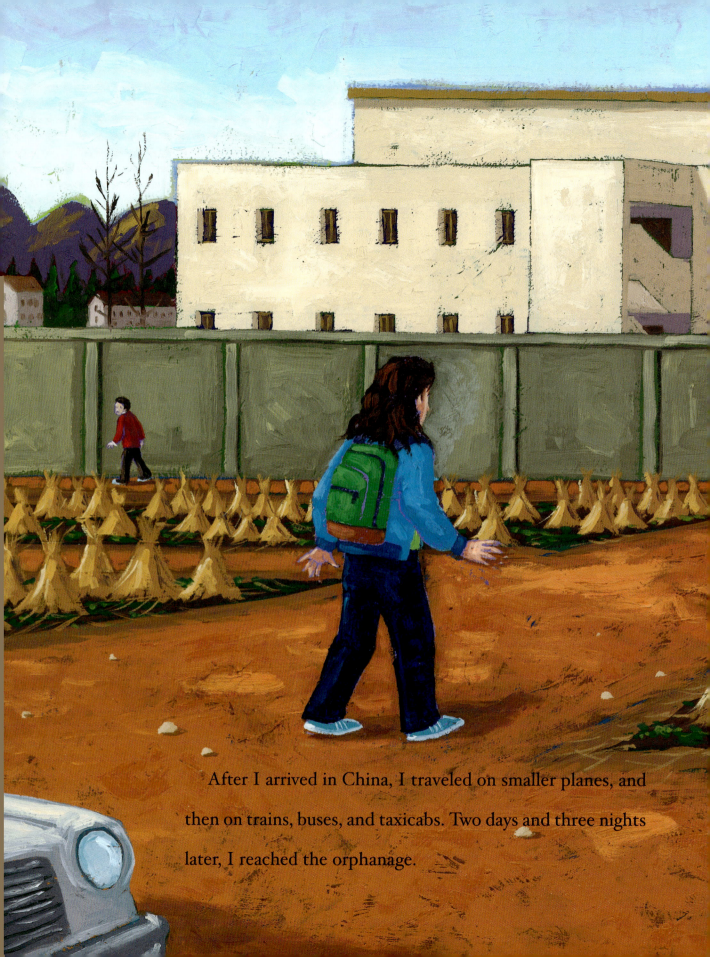

After I arrived in China, I traveled on smaller planes, and then on trains, buses, and taxicabs. Two days and three nights later, I reached the orphanage.

The square building was surrounded by a stone wall, set in
the middle of rice fields. The director welcomed me at the
gate and led me up the wide steps.

Inside the nursery, the caretakers lifted a baby from a cot where three others lay sleeping. "This is PanPan," they said.

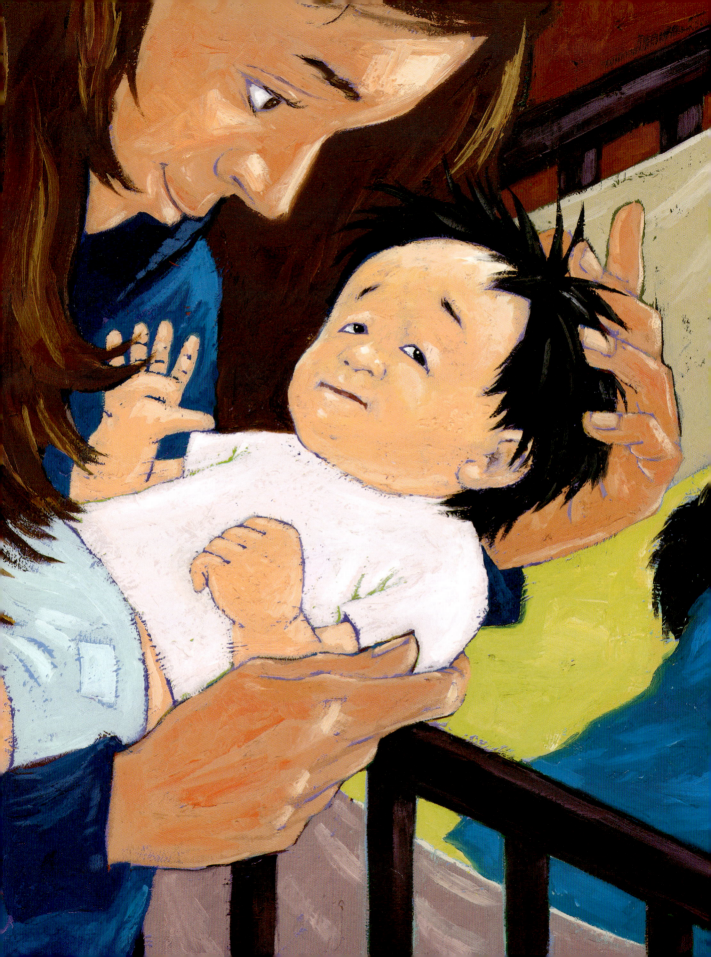

At last I held you in my arms! "Hello, my sweet girl," I said.

Though you were small and thin, you were very strong. I smiled at you, but you wouldn't meet my gaze, and you squirmed while I thanked the caretakers.

"She is a very good baby," they said.

"I know," I said.

The director waved good-bye, and I carried you to the waiting taxi.

When we reached our hotel room, I showed you the view of the city. You wriggled in my arms again, and I pulled you closer.

"This is new for me, too," I said. "I've never been here before, either." I pointed to the rooftops and to the wide river below. I described the fields and apple trees back home, and I told you all about Lily. "We'll be there soon," I said as I walked you inside.

But you weren't listening. Instead you looked around the room at the chair, the bed, the bureau, the curtains, the lamp, and the clock on the table. You looked everywhere but at me.

Everything in your life was different now. Where was your cot? Where were the other babies? Where were your caretakers? And who was this new person, carrying you around and pointing at things? You wriggled and squirmed and kicked your skinny little feet, and then you began to cry.

All day long I tried to comfort you. I gave you the milk formula. I showed you the rattle and the bear. You were hungry for the milk, but you pushed the toys away. I dressed you in the new clothes, but the pants and socks were too big, and you shook them off. I walked you back and forth, singing all the sweet lullabies I could remember. But they were unfamiliar melodies, and you couldn't understand the words. Nothing I did consoled you. You cried and cried until I felt like weeping, too, and by evening time, we were both very tired. I laid you down and bent to kiss you. You just turned your face away.

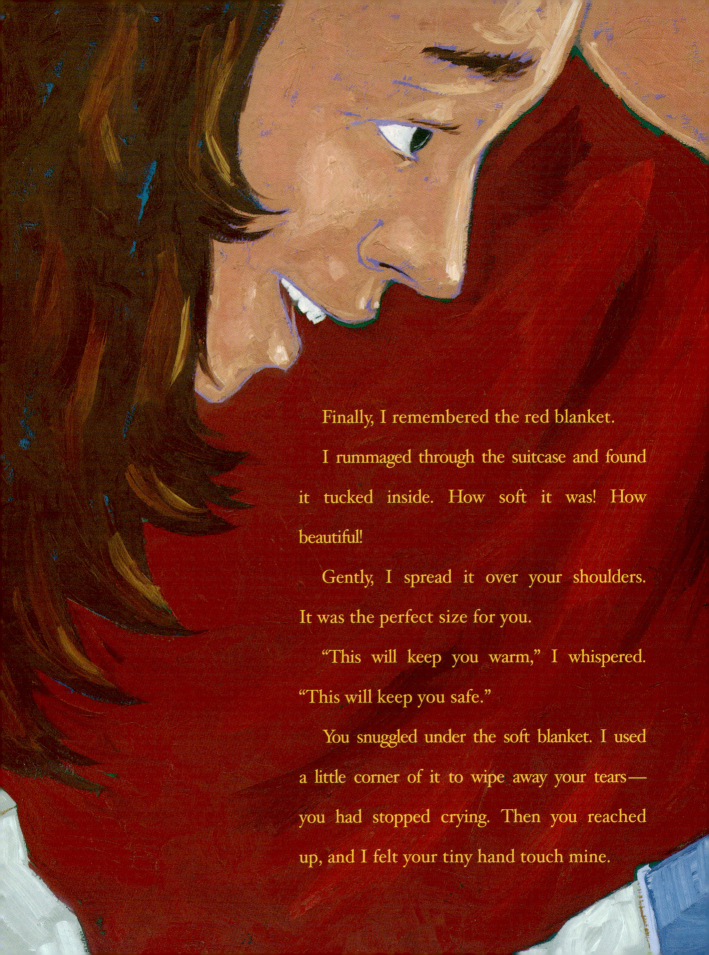

Finally, I remembered the red blanket.

I rummaged through the suitcase and found it tucked inside. How soft it was! How beautiful!

Gently, I spread it over your shoulders. It was the perfect size for you.

"This will keep you warm," I whispered. "This will keep you safe."

You snuggled under the soft blanket. I used a little corner of it to wipe away your tears— you had stopped crying. Then you reached up, and I felt your tiny hand touch mine.

Mother and daughter, we held on tight.

A few days later, we traveled home. Our friends and neighbors met us at the door. "Welcome home!" everybody cheered.

"Woof!" said Lily.

I carried you, bundled in the blanket, all around the house. "Here is our kitchen," I said. "And here is the living room and the piano. And look outside the window!" I pointed. "Apples! We will pick some tomorrow." Then I showed you your room. Together we looked at everything—the chair, the rug, the bureau, the curtains, the lamp, and the clock on the table. We looked at your crib, piled high with stuffed animals and toys that friends had brought for you. We looked at each other, and we smiled.

"I love you," I said.

We were very tired. We were very happy.

Now this house is filled with pictures you have drawn and books we read together and a beautiful piano we play every day. It no longer feels empty.

As I look at you, sitting at the kitchen table, I can hardly believe how much you have grown. You climb the apple trees and race around the yard with Lily. You have a new bike on the porch. You have a new, thick quilt on your bed. But every night, I still pull up the little red blanket as I hug and kiss you good night.

"Sweet dreams, my darling. I love you very much," I say. "You're the best thing that ever happened to me."

"I know," you say. "I love you, too."

And every morning, you bundle the blanket under your arm before you go out to play. When we take a weekend trip, it's the first thing you pack. You carry it with you everywhere. "It's special," you explain, if anyone asks.

The blanket is worn and faded by now, and some people think it's just a raggedy piece of cloth. But we know better, you and I. It will always be special. It will always be beautiful.

It will always be the soft, red blanket I brought you
long ago, on that magical day when we first became a
family.